ESCALADE

BY CADILLAC

A Crabtree Branches Book

Tracy Nelson Maurer

Crabtree Publishing

crabtreebooks.com

School-to-Home Support for Caregivers and Teachers

This high-interest book is designed to motivate striving students with engaging topics while building fluency, vocabulary, and an interest in reading. Here are a few questions and activities to help the reader build upon his or her comprehension skills.

Before Reading:

- *What do I think this book is about?*
- *What do I know about this topic?*
- *What do I want to learn about this topic?*
- *Why am I reading this book?*

During Reading:

- *I wonder why...*
- *I'm curious to know...*
- *How is this like something I already know?*
- *What have I learned so far?*

After Reading:

- *What was the author trying to teach me?*
- *What are some details?*
- *How did the photographs and captions help me understand more?*
- *Read the book again and look for the vocabulary words.*
- *What questions do I still have?*

Extension Activities:

- *What was your favorite part of the book? Write a paragraph on it.*
- *Draw a picture of your favorite thing you learned from the book.*

TABLE OF CONTENTS

SO STYLIN'

Superstars, kings and queens, and top-secret **VIPs** own the Cadillac Escalade for its swanky style. Some regular folks like its beefy look, too. But luxury doesn't come cheap. This Caddy costs from around $78,000 to well over $100,000.

For more than 100 years, Cadillac has been a **prestige** brand in the United States. Its famous crest is a symbol of wealth and taste to many people. When the Escalade rolled onto the streets in 1999, it revved up excitement for luxury **SUVs**.

Cadillac has a history of innovations. For example, Cadillac introduced the first electric starter in 1912. Drivers had to use hand cranks before this back-saving invention.

Tom Brady, David Beckham, and Adam Sandler are all Escalade owners.

SUPER SEATING

Over the years, Cadillac has updated the Escalade five times. In 2021, the company introduced hands-free driving and a newly designed cab that looks more like a fancy theater than a grocery-getter.

Interior lighting offers 19 color choices to set the mood.

Every Escalade features handcrafted leather seats, natural wood trim, and other fine details.

Look at that dashboard display! It's the first curved display of its kind with touch screen controls and richer colors than most home TVs.

The display panel has the broadest color range available in any vehicle so far.

Beyond the comfy heated and cooled seats, the Escalade also offers a listening experience that wraps the sound around each passenger. It's so good that singer James Blake has tested his songs in an Escalade before he has released them. Cadillac treated a small group of his fans to a private concert using the Escalade stereo system.

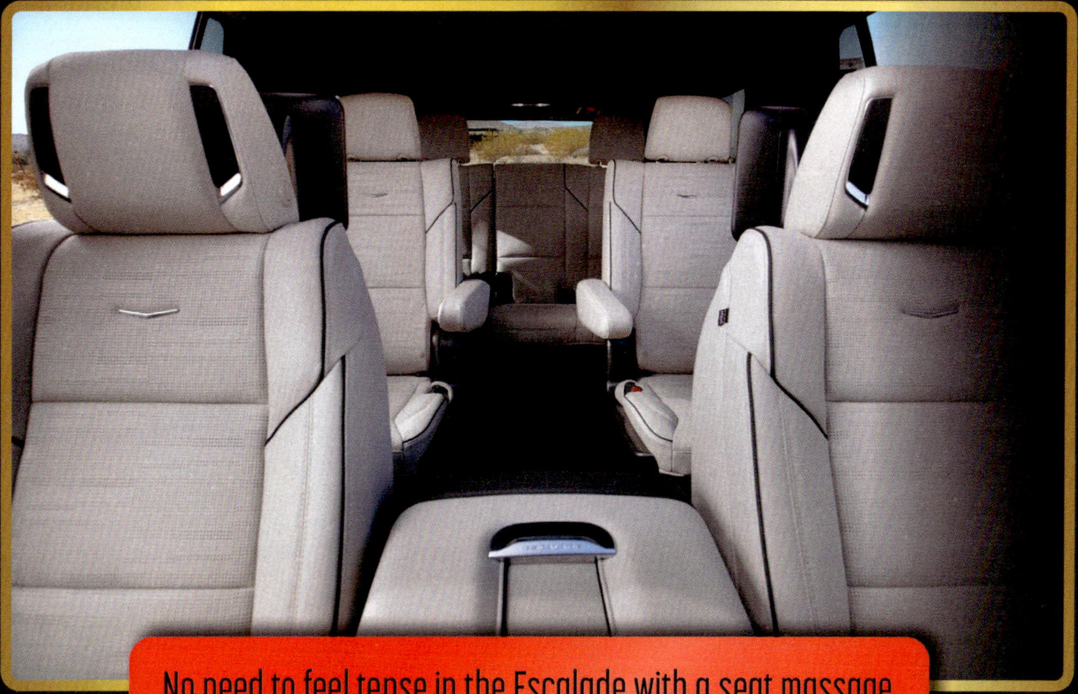

No need to feel tense in the Escalade with a seat massage.

COMFORT STRETCH

Cadillac stretched the 2021 Escalade to its longest length so far, giving the third row more legroom and opening up to 142 cubic feet (4 cubic meters) of **cargo** space—more than enough storage for a soccer team's gear.

Suspension controls let the driver lower the truck body for less of a step up into the truck. The truck body can also lift up for **clearance** on rough roads.

226.9 inches (756 cm) length

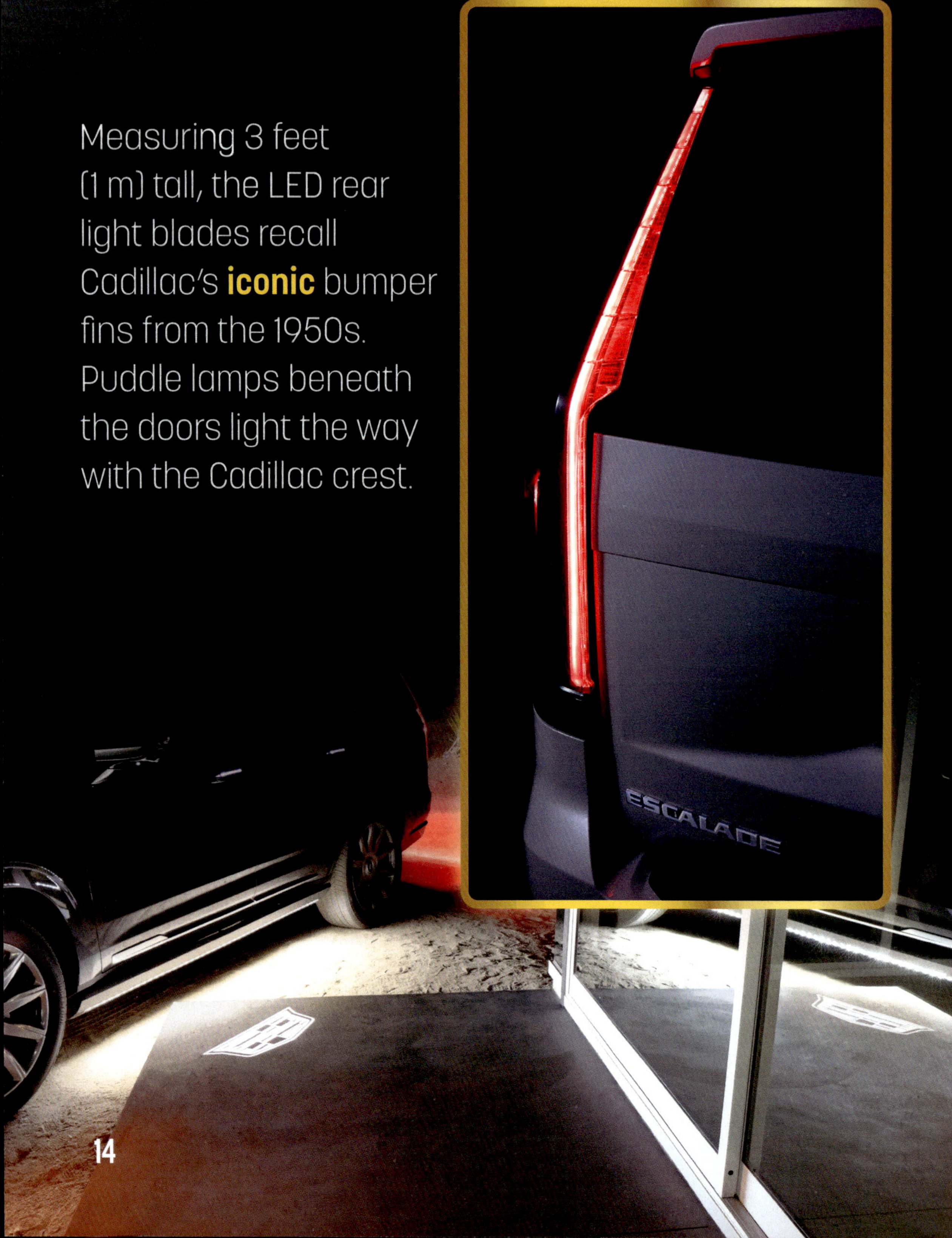

Measuring 3 feet (1 m) tall, the LED rear light blades recall Cadillac's **iconic** bumper fins from the 1950s. Puddle lamps beneath the doors light the way with the Cadillac crest.

BRIDGESTONE
ESCALADE

MUSCLE MACHINE

Even with all of its luxury dressing, the Escalade is still an SUV with a powerful engine. The standard 6.2-liter V8 engine delivers 420 **horsepower** and hefty towing muscle.

For the first time in the Escalade's history, Cadillac offered a diesel option in 2021. The 3.0-liter diesel engine features an inline six-cylinder setup with a **turbocharger**. Diesel engines usually last longer than gasoline engines and burn less fuel.

A V8 engine positions eight cylinders in a V shape to burn fuel. An inline six-cylinder motor burns fuel in six cylinders set up in a single row.

An optional control system under the vehicle reads every inch of the road 1,000 times per second to respond to uneven surfaces. That's one smooth ride.

EYES ON THE ROAD

Safety matters on the road and in the parking lot. The Escalade uses many cameras to show an overhead picture of the entire area around the vehicle.

3D Overhead
74° 1:44
ON
AUTO
OFF
A/C
SYNC
START
ENGINE
STOP

3D Overhead

Escalade drivers can see better in the dark. The Night Vision option senses heat to create an image of people or large animals beyond the headlamps.

0
MPH
3
4
5
6
RPMx1000
E
154mi

DELUXE LUXURY

Some people want luxury on top of luxury! **Specialty** companies turn Escalades into rides that double as office suites or party rooms for wealthy clients. Interiors with extra-large TVs, footrests for each seat, or cabinets for glassware add a fancy touch. Exterior upgrades might include extra glossy black paint, blacked-out grills, tinted windows, or shiny chrome accents.

Some companies turn Escalades into stretch limousines.

Luxury can also mean extra security. **Armor** technology such as bulletproof windows, electric-shock door handles, and pepper spray nozzles mounted on the roof offer mega protection. These rides cost about $350,000.

P 888
PT 54

AN ELECTRIC ESCALADE?

Critics say the Escalade guzzles too much gas. They do suck up fuel! These SUVs typically get about 15 miles (24 km) per gallon with city driving and 20 miles (32 km) per gallon on the highway. Cadillac may release the Escalade as an electric vehicle someday.

No matter how it changes in the future, the Escalade is the SUV to watch for American luxury.

GLOSSARY

armor (AHR-mur): Protective gear

cargo (KAHR-goh): Transported items

clearance (KLEER-uhns): Space between the ground and vehicle

critics (KRIT-iks): People who find something wrong with things

horsepower (HORS-pou-ur): A unit for measuring an engine's power

iconic (EYE-kohn-ik): A well-known symbol

prestige (pre-STEEEZH): A high standing based on respect or credit from others

specialty (SPESH-uhl-tee): Focused on certain skills, products, or services

SUVs (ESS-YOU-VEEZ): An abbreviation for Sport Utility Vehicles

turbocharger (TUR-boh-CHARJ-ur): A device that pushes extra air into an engine for more power

VIPs (VEE-EYE-PEEZ): An abbreviation for Very Important Persons

INDEX

WEBSITES TO VISIT

https://www.cadillac.com

https://www.guideautoweb.com/en/galleries/54082/the-cadillac-escalade-through-time/?im=11

https://beckerautodesign.com/esv/index.html

https://www.motortrend.com/news/2021-cadillac-escalade-duramax-diesel-engine-details/

ABOUT THE AUTHOR

Tracy Nelson Maurer

Tracy Nelson Maurer has written more than 100 nonfiction books for young readers. She lives in Minnesota where she happily drives a minivan.

Crabtree Publishing

crabtreebooks.com 800-387-7650

Produced by: Blue Door Education for Crabtree Publishing
Written by: Tracy Nelson Maurer
Designed by: Jennifer Dydyk
Edited by: Kelli Hicks
Proofreader: Janine Deschenes

Hardcover	978-1-4271-5483-5
Paperback	978-1-4271-5489-7
Ebook (pdf)	978-1-4271-5495-8
Epub	978-1-4271-5501-6
Read-along	978-1-4271-5507-8
Audio book	978-1-4271-5513-9

Printed in Canada/102023/CPC20231018

Published in Canada
Crabtree Publishing
616 Welland Avenue
St. Catharines, Ontario
L2M 5V6

Published in the United States
Crabtree Publishing
347 Fifth Avenue
Suite 1402-145
New York, NY 10016

Photographs: Cover: Logo graphic © Shutterstock.com/officeku, speedometer © Shutterstock.com/Panuwatccn, shiny car hood top left on cover and throughout book © Shutterstock.com/ Inked Pixels, Escalade cover photo © Cadillac.com. All Rights Reserved, Title page : ©Cadillac.com. All Rights Reserved, PG 4: ©Cadillac.com. All Rights Reserved, PG 5: ©Cadillac.com (top), Tom Brady © All-Pro Reels from District of Columbia, USA https:// creativecommons, org/licenses/by-sa/2.0/deed.en. ©Andrea Raffin / Shutterstock.com, ©Kathy Hutchins / Shutterstock. com, PG 6-7: ©Cadillac.com (all). All Rights Reserved, PG 8-9: ©Cadillac.com (all). All Rights Reserved, PG 10-11: ©Cadillac.com (all). All Rights Reserved, PG 12-13: ©Cadillac.com (all). All Rights Reserved, PG 14-15: ©Cadillac.com (all). All Rights Reserved, PG 16-17: ©Cadillac.com (all). All Rights Reserved, PG 18-19: ©Cadillac. com. All Rights Reserved, PG 19: ©Kanison| Dreamstime.com (inset), PG 20-21: ©Cadillac.com (all). All Rights Reserved, PG 22-23: ©Cadillac.com (all). All Rights Reserved, PG 24: ©Brphoto| Dreamstime.com, PG 25: ©Art Konovalov / Shutterstock.com, PG 26-27: ©Yelenapilipchuk| Dreamstime.com, PG 28: ©Art Konovalov / Shutterstock.com, PG 29: ©Valokuva24 / Shutterstock.com (top), ©Cadillac.com. All Rights Reserved. Special Thanks to cadillac.com for the use of their images to teach young children reading skills using nonfiction/editorial informational text and images.

Library and Archives Canada Cataloguing in Publication

Title: Escalade by Cadillac / Tracy Nelson Maurer.
Names: Maurer, Tracy Nelson, 1965- author.
Description: Series statement: Luxury rides | "A Crabtree branches book". Includes index.
Identifiers: Canadiana (print) 20210220562 | Canadiana (ebook) 20210220570 | ISBN 9781427154835 (hardcover) | ISBN 9781427154897 (softcover) | ISBN 9781427154958 (HTML) | ISBN 9781427155016 (EPUB) | ISBN 9781427155078 (read-along ebook)
Subjects: LCSH: Escalade sport utility vehicle—Juvenile literature.
Classification: LCC TL215.C27 M38 2022 | DDC j629.222/2—dc23

Library of Congress Cataloging-in-Publication Data

Names: Maurer, Tracy Nelson, 1965- author.
Title: Escalade by Cadillac / Tracy Nelson Maurer.
Description: New York : Crabtree Publishing Company, [2022] Series:Luxury rides | "A Crabtree branches book." | Includes bibliographical references and index.
Identifiers: LCCN 2021022089 (print) | LCCN 2021022090 (ebook) | ISBN 9781427154835 (hardcover) | ISBN 9781427154897 (paperback) | ISBN 9781427154958 (ebook) | ISBN 9781427155016 (epub) | ISBN 9781427155078
Subjects: LCSH: Escalade sport utility vehicle--Juvenile literature.
Classification: LCC TL230.5.E785 M38 2022 (print) | LCC TL230.5.E785 (ebook) | DDC 629.223--dc23
LC record available at https://lccn.loc.gov/2021022089
LC ebook record available at https://lccn.loc.gov/2021022090